# How Many Candles?

Written by Stevie Ann Wilde
Illustrated by Karen Hayles

## Collins Educational
*An imprint of HarperCollinsPublishers*

I am 1.
One candle on the birthday cake.

I am 2.
Two candles on the birthday cake.

I am 3.

Three candles on the birthday cake.

I am 4.
Four candles on the birthday cake.

I am 5.
Five candles on the birthday cake.

I am 6.
Six candles on the birthday cake.

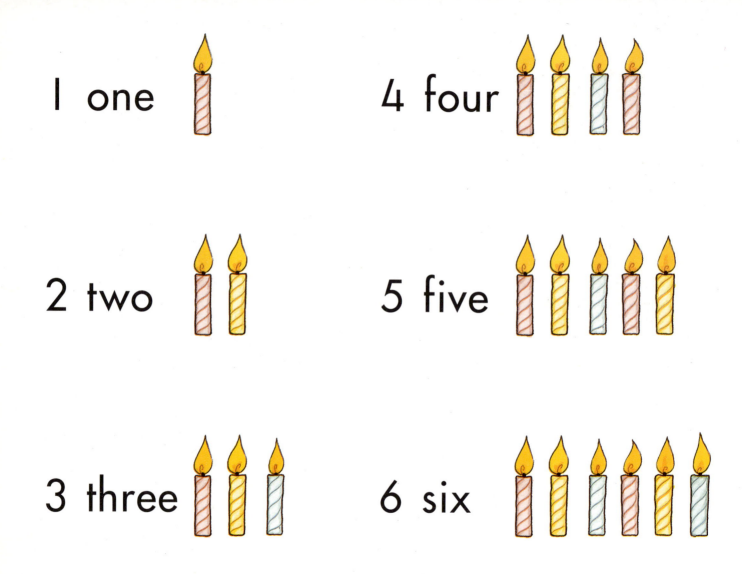

Big Ed is new.
But I am not a fan of his!
He will be bad for the team!

But if we win,
Big Ed tells us *he* did it!

But if the Rams do not win …

Grrrrr! The Rams suck!

Big Ed gets mad and kicks up a big fuss.

Big Ed is not a team player. He cannot be in the Rams team. He has to go!